anythink

# Tyrion's Tale

# A Story for Kids About a Rescue Dog

D1441576

By Tyrion Pittister

As Told to Laurie Holding

ISBN-13: 978-1727494044
ISBN-10: 1727494040

## Disclaimer

The authors and publishers make no warranty, express or implied, that the information contained herein is appropriate for every individual, situation or purpose, and assume no responsibility for errors or omissions. The reader assumes the risk and full responsibility for all actions, and the authors will not be held responsible for any loss or damage, whether consequential, incidental, special or otherwise that may result from the information presented in this publication.

At the time of Tyrion's rescue, no photographs were permitted due to legal proceedings involving his handlers. We have, for the purpose of Story, inserted pictures of current veterinarians, techs, and groomers to depict what actually happened to him in those early days of his freedom.

Here's how you say my name: Tee-Ree-Un.

Look at me!

This is what I look like. Some people get scared when they see me.
They think I'm going to bite them, because I look snarly.
Other people think I look like I'm smiling all the time.
They point at me and laugh.

Some of my teeth are missing. (Look at the bottom ones!)

And I only have half of a tail.

This is me.

I don't care what people think. I just want to kiss everyone.
I love them all.

I love kids the best, because they're shorter and their voices are high.

I **don't** like it when they hug me. (Dogs don't like the feeling of being squeezed. It makes most of us nervous.)

But I love a good juicy kiss.

I used to live in a yard full of dogs. None of us had enough to eat and there wasn't fresh water. It was too hot to be out in the sun all day. Nobody loved us. And the people chained us up so we were all stuck there. Life was really hard.

But then, one day, a whole bunch of people came busting into the yard, and took all of us away in trucks! I was scared because of the noise and commotion. It was a big day.

And what happened was I got a bubbly bath. And good food. And clean, fresh water. All for the very first time.

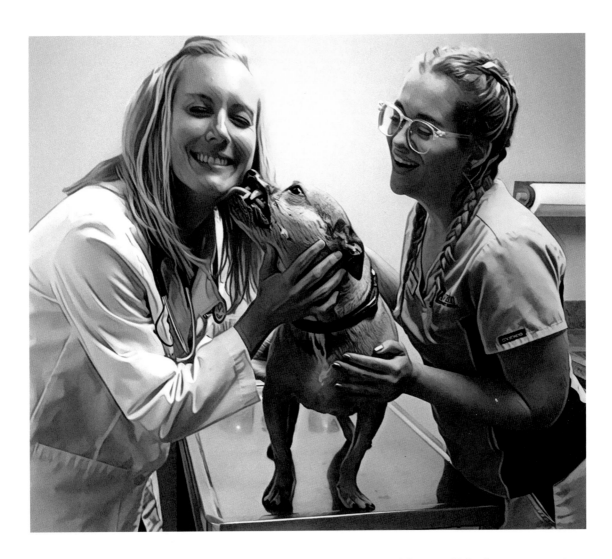

That's when I saw my very first doctor. And boy, did she see me! I got lots of prickly shots and a lot of my sore spots got medicine. I kissed her and stole treats from her apron pockets with a flick of my very long tongue. It made her laugh. Hers was the very first laugh I had ever heard.

They let me sleep in my own little space, like a little cave made out of metal. I was cool and clean and full for the very first time. It was amazing.

One day, two pretty women came all the way down to Florida from Pennsylvania to take me away. Just me! They talked nice and soft to me, and I rode in my special cave bed, snoozing most of the trip away. That's when I tasted pumpkin for the very first time. And boy, did I love that stuff. Here's a picture of one of the women, Sally, holding me.

The women drove me to my very first house. I saw stairs for the very first time. But I didn't know how to do them.

The next day, though, it was back in the car. The women took me to their people all the way up in Pittsburgh, Pennsylvania. These people only rescue Pit Bulls. And that's what I am. Lucky me! This is Daisy. She's the leader of the rescue.

The people at the rescue place were really kind. They understood when I had potty accidents. They knew I had never been inside anywhere, so I just didn't know where to do those potty things. They had good food. I got fresh water all through the day, and three square meals. Sometimes they even gave me a toy called a Kong. Inside it was frozen pumpkin and peanut butter. My favorite tastes, even now.

The rescue people raised enough money for me to get an operation on my nose. I couldn't breathe very well back then, so I couldn't smell, either. I was missing out.

After the operation, I looked even more different than before! They had to take away part of my nose. But suddenly, I could smell! I smelled other dogs at the rescue place. I smelled the people who came to walk me and feed me and teach me some manners. I smelled pumpkin and peanut butter. I smelled apples and grass being mowed outside and I smelled deer far, far away. These were my very first smells.

One day, a woman and her daughter came to the rescue. They wanted to foster a dog. Some people foster dogs because their hearts are so big that they want to save lots of lives, not just one. Foster parents make a space in their house for you and feed you and help work on your manners, and then when you get adopted, your foster parents take in another dog and start all over.

So off I went to my foster house. Besides the woman and the daughter, there was also a man and a son.

I was still working on my manners, but that very first night, the man of the house made steak, which is the very best smell in the world. I was so excited about that smell that I leaped up onto the kitchen table and ate a huge hunk from his plate. Everyone screamed and laughed all at once. I kissed them. The steak was juicy and delicious.

I liked living in the big house. It was the biggest house I'd ever seen. Lots of stairs. I didn't want to do the stairs after I fell down them that very first day, so nobody ever made me go back up there again. And really, why bother, when the food isn't even up there.

There were places in the house where I could lie down and watch deer walk by the windows. Turkeys came to the door looking for corn. Woodpeckers made big knocking sounds in the woods. There were so many great smells I lost count.

I got two delicious meals every day and here's what I got: pumpkin, watermelon, apple, banana, kibbles, shredded carrots, and sometimes a couple bites of real meat. Here's a picture of one of my actual dinners.

After a couple of weeks in the woods, my foster people decided to adopt me. They loved me, they said! They couldn't say goodbye to me, they said! They called me a "good boy" even when I still had potty accidents inside the house, or when I broke into that gigantic bag of red licorice.

Turns out the son and the daughter were grown up enough to live on their own. They moved to a little house together. My new mom and dad and I moved away, too.

We moved to a little village with sidewalks and neighbors and water bowls for thirsty dogs outside the shops. My house has a fenced-in yard, so I can lie in the sunshine any time I want. Or I can go in (through my brand-new doggie door!) when I get too hot. I get to choose!

Mom and Dad take me for walks, and pet me, and feed me treats all day long. They kiss me and tell me I'm beautiful. Which I already knew. Dad bought me this stroller for my birthday since my legs are limpy and I can't walk too far without having to sit down.

Now I have a job, and that's to help other dogs, especially Pit Bulls like me, who might be chained up in hot yards with no water and no food like I was. I help my rescuers who helped me, spreading the word that people should always treat their dogs with respect, and I raise money so they can do their jobs saving Pit Bulls.

This is me at my birthday party, raising money. They have it at a restaurant and lots of people come. I get my own cake! But the money goes to the rescue.

Look at me. I may not be the most handsome dog, but that doesn't matter. I may not have had the happiest beginning, but that doesn't matter, either. All that matters is that we love ourselves enough to love others. When we stop judging people and animals by what they look like, we end up forgetting about our own scars, too.

Look at me. Look at love.

The End

A portion of the profits from sales of this book will go to Hello Bully, the rescue who helped save my life and who helped me find my forever family. You can follow me on my Facebook page (Tyrion Pittister) and you can help dogs like me by donating to Hello Bully on their website: www.hellobully.com.

Made in the USA
Coppell, TX
01 March 2020

16375163R00021